Trees

June Loves

Chelsea House Publishers
2080 Cabot Boulevard West, Suite 201
Langhorne, PA 19047-1813

The Chelsea House world wide web address is www.chelseahouse.com

First published in 2005 by
MACMILLAN EDUCATION AUSTRALIA PTY LTD
627 Chapel Street, South Yarra, Australia 3141

Visit our website at www.macmillan.com.au

Associated companies and representatives throughout the world.

Library of Congress Cataloging-in-Publication Data
Loves, June.
    Trees / June Loves.
    p. cm. – (Plants)
    Includes index.
    ISBN 0-7910-8268-7
    1. Trees – Juvenile literature. I. Title.
    QK475.8.L68 2005
    582.16–dc22

                                             2004016339

Edited by Anna Fern
Text and cover design by Christine Deering
Page layout by Christine Deering
Photo research by Legend Images
Illustrations by Melissa Webb

Printed in China

Acknowledgements

The author and the publisher are grateful to the following for permission to reproduce
copyright material:

Cover photograph: Sequoia forest, courtesy of Corbis Digital Stock.

Jean-Paul Ferrero/AUSCAPE, pp. 21, 27; Rob Walls/AUSCAPE, p. 11; Australian
Picture Library, p. 30; Corbis Digital Stock, pp. 1, 7, 9; The DW Stock Picture Library,
pp. 15 (left), 18, 29; Getty Images, pp. 12, 14 (top and bottom); Getty Images/
Photodisc, p. 16; Jiri Lochman/Lochman Transparencies, p. 20; Len Stewart/Lochman
Transparencies, p. 13; Photodisc, pp. 4, 5, 8 (left and right), 15 (right), 17, 22, 26;
Photolibrary.com, pp. 3, 10, 19; Steve Lovegrove/Picture Tasmania Photo Library, pp.
6, 8 (centre), 23, 28.

While every care has been taken to trace and acknowledge copyright, the publisher
tenders their apologies for any accidental infringement where copyright has proved
untraceable. Where the attempt has been unsuccessful, the publisher welcomes
information that would redress the situation.

Contents

Plants

Plants are living things. They grow all over the world, in hot and cold places.

Some plants can survive in cold winter snows.

Trees

Trees are the tallest plants of all. They have a woody trunk. Some trees are huge and have long branches.

Trees provide homes and food for many insects, birds, and animals.

Where Trees Grow

Trees grow in forests in most parts of the world. They grow in **tropical rain forests** where it is hot and wet. Some trees have **roots** that can grow where there is a lot of water.

These mangrove trees grow with their roots in water.

Trees grow in cool forests. Some trees drop their
leaves in fall. Pine trees grow well in very cold places.

Tree roots stop the soil from wearing away.

Kinds of Trees

There are two main kinds of trees:

- conifers
- broad-leaved trees.

This is a broad-leaved tree.   This is a conifer.

Conifers

Most conifer trees, such as pines, firs, cedars, and redwoods, grow their seeds in hard, woody cones. Different conifers have different needle-like leaves that grow in patterns.

Giant sequoia trees are conifers. They are the tallest living plants.

Broad-leaved Trees

Most broad-leaved trees have flowers and wide, flat leaves. Some broad-leaved trees, called deciduous trees, lose their leaves in fall. Many **fruit** trees are broad-leaved trees.

Some broad-leaved trees lose their leaves in the fall.

Broad-leaved trees produce flowers and develop seeds. The seeds are often enclosed in a hard nut or a fleshy fruit.

Many fruit trees are broad-leaved trees.

Parts of Trees

The leaves of trees collect energy from the sun to make food inside the tree. The roots of trees hold the tree in place, and collect water and **nutrients** from the soil.

leaves

branches

bark

woody trunk

leaf litter returns nutrients to the soil

roots

The olive tree is a broad-leaved tree that is grown for its fruit.

Inside the fruit there are seeds from which new trees will grow.

Inside each olive there is a seed.

How Trees Grow

Most trees grow from seeds. A seed contains a tiny plant and a storage of food to help the tree grow.

A seed sprouts a root and a **shoot**. The root grows down into the earth, and the shoot grows up towards the sun. Gradually the shoot becomes a stem, and the stem grows leaves.

In time, the thin stem will grow into a strong tree trunk with branches.

The tree flowers and makes fruits or cones containing seeds for new trees.

A tree makes a new ring of wood each year. You can count the rings in an old tree stump to find out how old the tree was.

How a Flowering Tree Makes Seeds

Flowers have female parts and male parts. The female parts contain tiny eggs. The male parts produce a special dust, called **pollen**. The eggs need to join with some pollen so the tree can produce fruit and seeds.

eggs are hidden here (female parts)

pollen (male parts)

When the bee feeds from the apple blossom, it will pick up some pollen on its furry body.

Some flowers contain **nectar**, which attracts insects and birds. While the insect drinks the nectar, pollen falls onto it. The insect carries the pollen to the eggs of the next flower that it visits. This is called **pollination**.

After pollination the female parts of the flower grow into a fruit containing seeds.

How a Conifer Makes Seeds

Conifers produce seeds in their woody cones rather than in flowers. Pine trees grow small female cones containing eggs. They also grow male cones, called yellow catkins, which make pollen.

A catkin releases clouds of dusty pollen in the wind.

The pollen from the catkins scatters into the air and lands on the female cone. The pollen joins with the eggs inside the female cone. Seeds then grow in the cone. When the cone turns brown and woody, the seeds are released.

The seeds from the pinecones grow into new trees.

Helpers for Traveling Seeds

Seeds from trees are carried away by wind, water, and animals. Some seeds are inside fruit. Animals or birds eat the fruit and drop the seeds. Even if an animal eats the seed, the seed can still grow out of an animal's droppings.

Orangutans spread the seeds of the fruit they eat.

Sycamore seeds are carried by the wind. The seeds have wings to help them fly. Coconuts are the seeds of palm trees. Coconuts float on water. When they are washed up on a beach they begin to sprout and grow.

A coconut can travel a long way on water before it starts to grow.

Growing Trees

Planting a tree can be a lot of fun. You need to dig a hole with a spade for the tree. Once you have planted the tree you need to water it well.

Many people enjoy growing fruit trees in their garden.

Trees, like most plants, need soil, water, and light to grow well. A layer of **mulch** helps keep the soil moist and helps stop weeds from growing.

A layer of mulch helps stop tree roots from drying out.

Grow an Avocado Tree

Save the stone of an avocado and watch it grow.

What you need:

- avocado stone
- four toothpicks
- jar
- water
- pot
- soil

What to do:

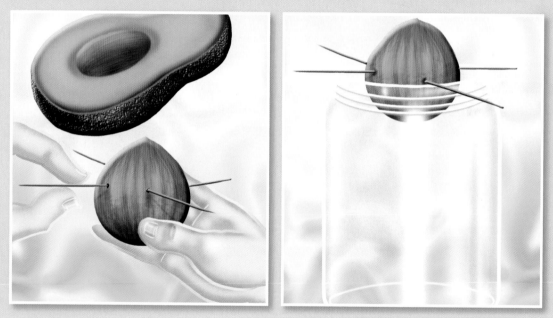

1 Stick three or four toothpicks into the avocado stone.

2 Rest the stone on top of the jar, pointed end up.

3 Fill the jar with water and put it on a warm, sunny windowsill. In about one month, the stone will sprout and grow roots.

4 Plant your avocado tree in a pot with soil and watch it grow.

Tips for Gardeners

You can grow trees from seeds.

- Plant tree seeds in pots and water them every day.

- When your tree is a good size, replant it in a larger pot or plant it in the garden.

When the roots are tangled like this, the tree is ready for a bigger pot.

- Many trees can grow to be very tall. Make sure you choose the right tree for the right place.

- Always wash your hands and scrub your nails when you have finished handling soil.

Huge trees such as these eucalypts grow from tiny seeds.

Useful Trees

Trees provide food such as fruit, nuts, and maple syrup. Some trees are grown on farms to produce crops to eat.

Apples and pears are delicious fruits grown on trees.

Trees grown in forests are used to make products such as paper, or timber for buildings, furniture, and musical instruments. The **sap** from some trees, such as rubber trees, is used to make many useful things.

The sap being milked from this rubber tree will be used to make all sorts of rubber products.

Amazing Trees

Trees are the giants of the plant world.

- The tallest plant is the giant sequoia tree. It can grow 270 feet (80 meters) high.

- The largest seed, weighing up to 44 pounds (20 kilograms), comes from the double coconut palm.

- The longest leaves of any plant belong to the raphia palm. They can grow up to 66 feet (20 meters) long.

This is a double coconut palm seed.

Glossary

fruit	part of a flowering plant that contains seeds
leaf litter	a layer of fallen leaves
mulch	a layer of chopped-up leaves or other plant material to help stop the soil from drying out and stop weeds from growing
nectar	sweet liquid made by flowers which attracts animals and insects
nutrients	food in the soil that a plant can use to grow
pollen	fine yellow dust made in the center of a flower
pollination	movement of pollen from one flower to another
tropical rain forest	a thick forest where the weather is warm and wet, and which is full of living things
root	part of a plant that grows down into the soil and takes in water and nutrients
sap	a sticky liquid from inside a tree
shoot	young branch or stem of a plant

Index